Space—
and People's Ideas About Space

by Israel Walker

Editorial Offices: Glenview, Illinois • Parsippany, New Jersey • New York, New York
Sales Offices: Needham, Massachusetts • Duluth, Georgia • Glenview, Illinois
Coppell, Texas • Sacramento, California • Mesa, Arizona

The Big Dipper is a group of stars that looks like the shape of a water cup with a handle for dipping the cup into water.

Ancient Studies of Space

Since the time of the first humans, people have looked at space in many ways and for many reasons. Two of the ways we will consider in this book are the scientific exploration of space and fictional stories about life in space. People have studied space scientifically, gathering information by observing facts and testing ideas. They also have told made-up stories about space.

Ancient people looked at the stars in the sky. They saw groups of stars that looked like the shapes of objects. They also studied the stars to predict changes of the seasons, so farmers knew when to plant their crops. Ancient people sometimes made up stories about the groups of stars. These early studies of the stars were a mix of science and fictional stories.

---

ancient: of times long ago

Our Solar System

telescope

Galileo Galilei's greatest gift to science was the use of the telescope to observe space.

Astronomy: Scientific Study of Space

The first modern astronomer, or space scientist, was Nicolaus Copernicus. He was a Polish scientist. In 1514, he developed the theory (or explanation) that the Sun, not the Earth, was the center of our Solar System. His theory helped people understand our universe. It also helped other astronomers in their studies.

In 1610, an Italian astronomer named Galileo Galilei was the first person to use a telescope to prove Copernicus's theory that the Sun was the center of the Solar System. Telescopes helped astronomers see farther into space. But telescopes had to be improved greatly before astronomers could see all eight planets of our Solar System.

The astronauts Neil Armstrong and Edwin Aldrin on the surface of the Moon

Human Space Travel

During the 1950s, scientists started to study the idea of sending space ships with humans into space. The United States began a space program managed by the National Aeronautics and Space Administration (NASA). Another country, the Soviet Union, sent the first human into space, on April 12, 1961. The Russian astronaut Yuri Gagarin orbited the Earth in a spacecraft. This made the world realize that human space travel was possible. Just 23 days later, the United Sates sent a spacecraft with Alan Shepard into space.

A space race had begun. Which country would be the first to send someone to the Moon? On July 20, 1969, NASA astronauts Neil Armstrong and Edwin ("Buzz") Aldrin, of the United States, landed and walked on the Moon.

---

orbited: went around

The Hubble Space Telescope orbits (travels around) the Earth.

Other Scientific Studies

NASA continued to develop new ways to study space. More astronauts went into space and to the Moon. Astronauts gathered moon rocks and practiced moving outside of the spacecraft. Scientists studied the effects of living in space. NASA created a spacecraft so that it could take off and land many times, instead of being used only once.

NASA also launched many satellites and unmanned spacecraft. Weather satellites orbit the Earth. They record storm patterns from space, allowing weather forecasters to be aware of dangerous storms. Satellites can also take pictures of farms, showing farmers which fields need water. Since 1990, the Hubble Space Telescope has been orbiting the Earth. It takes pictures of distant galaxies for scientists to study.

---

satellites: objects made by humans orbiting around objects in space

unmanned: controlled without a person onboard

galaxies: groups of stars and planets

International Space Station

In 1977, NASA sent *Voyager 1* and *Voyager 2,* two unmanned spacecraft, to study and take pictures of the outer planets (Jupiter, Saturn, Uranus, and Neptune).

In 2004, NASA sent small vehicles called rovers to explore the surface of Mars. Mars is the closest planet to Earth. Many scientists believe there was water on Mars at some point in history. They believe a planet that had water also may have had living things. Scientists are eager to study Mars.

Together with other countries from all over the world, Russia and the United States constructed a huge station in space where astronauts and scientists are able to live and study. This is called the International Space Station. It is the size of a football field. The first crew arrived at the station in the year 2000, and people have lived and worked there ever since.

New Space Studies

Scientists called astrobiologists study the possibility of life on other planets. What they have learned indicates that Earth is the only planet in our Solar System capable of supporting life. The other planets are too hot or too cold. However, scientists also know that there are billions of stars in our universe. Some stars are the centers of their own solar systems, with planets. Astrobiologists are studying the other solar systems to see if any planets seem capable of supporting life.

Could there be life in other solar systems? Astrobiologists are trying to find the answer.

Are There Intelligent Beings Far from Earth?

A project called SETI (the Search for Extra-Terrestrial Intelligence) scientifically searches for life on other planets. SETI scientists use antennas to record signals coming from outer space. Using powerful computers, SETI scientists then examine the signals and try to determine if any of those signals come from intelligent living beings. SETI scientists believe that it is possible that other planets in the universe support life.

Some scientists believe the people who work at SETI are wrong. These scientists believe SETI is not conducting scientific research.

The SETI Institute uses this radio telescope in Puerto Rico to search for radio signals from outer space.

Artists have made pictures of the kinds of space ships and flying machines that appear in science fiction.

Science Fiction

Space exploration inspired the imaginations of many people. Since ancient times, people have told stories about space adventures. In modern times, people write stories, books, and plays about imaginary space exploration. This kind of writing is known as science fiction because it uses ideas that are based on scientific discoveries and often includes space travel.

A famous example of science fiction writing is the radio play called "The War of the Worlds," performed in 1938. At that time, people did not have televisions. People listened to music and plays on the radio.

---

fiction: invented stories

Orson Welles

Orson Welles, a famous radio actor, made a version of "The War of the Worlds," a book by H.G. Wells, to perform on the radio. The play was about an attack on the world by aliens from Mars. Some people listening to the radio thought the play was true. They believed the world was being attacked by aliens. They packed their bags and ran onto the streets. They were trying to get away from the aliens. Radio announcers had to explain that the play was only fiction, and that there was no real invasion by aliens from Mars. Policemen went out into the streets to explain that the play was only fiction. Soon the panic ended. But people realized just how powerful science fiction writing could be.

---

panic: terror, great fear

Many people enjoy dressing up as aliens.

Science Fiction in Our Time

There have been many popular science fiction writers. Today, many movies have stories about aliens, space travel, or the future of the world. Some stories explore what aliens will look like. Others show whole civilizations in space where humans and aliens live together in peace or in trouble. Many people enjoy science fiction. Men, women, and children read science fiction stories, imagining what the world might be like someday or somewhere far away.

Extend Language   Plural Nouns

To make most nouns plural, you add an -s to the end of words such as, *author*. *Author* and -s make the plural noun *authors*. When a word ends in *sh, ch, x, s,* and *z*, you add an -es to make the plural noun. For example: *branch* becomes *branches.*

Can you find examples of plural nouns in this book?

Space: Room for the Imagination

For thousands of years, people have been inspired by the night sky. Ancient people studied the stars. They noticed that the stars appeared at certain times of the year. People began to use the stars like a calendar. They also created fictional stories about heroes and heroines of the sky. We can say that these ancient discoveries and stories about stars were the first astronomy and the first science fiction.

Now scientists and authors around the world continue these traditions. Scientists study the movements of stars, planets, and other bodies in space. Authors write about life in outer space. Scientists and writers continue to find new ways of exploring space.